RICK CITY LIBRARY

WITHDRAWN FROM STOCK

WITHDRAWN FROM STOCK

D0487637

Quick and Easy Crafts

Decorative Painting

Quick and Easy Crafts

Decorative Painting

15 step-by-step projects – simple to make, stunning results

STEPHANIE WEIGHTMAN

NEW
HOLLAND

745/723

35089
PUBLIC LIBRARY

Dedication

This book is dedicated to the memory of my Mum, who remains my inspiration and will be forever in my heart and soul.

First published in 2004 by
New Holland Publishers (UK) Ltd
London · Cape Town · Sydney · Auckland

Garfield House, 86–88 Edgware Road, London W2 2EA, United Kingdom
www.newhollandpublishers.com

80 McKenzie Street, Cape Town 8001, South Africa

Level 1, Unit 4, 14 Aquatic Drive, Frenchs Forest, NSW 2086, Australia

218 Lake Road, Northcote, Auckland, New Zealand

Copyright © 2004 text and project designs: Stephanie Weightman
Copyright © 2004 photographs: New Holland Publishers (UK) Ltd
Copyright © 2004 New Holland Publishers (UK) Ltd

All rights reserved. No part of this publication may be reproduced, stored in a retrieval system, or transmitted in any form or by any means, electronic, mechanical, photocopying, recording or otherwise, without the prior written permission of the publishers and copyright holders.

Stephanie Weightman has asserted her moral right to be identified as the author of this work.

ISBN 1 84330 692 1

Senior Editor: Clare Sayer
Production: Hazel Kirkman
Design: AG&G Books Glyn Bridgewater
Photographer: Shona Wood
Editorial Direction: Rosemary Wilkinson

10 9 8 7 6 5 4 3 2 1

Reproduction by Pica Digital PTE Ltd, Singapore
Printed and bound by Times Offset (M) Sdn Bhd, Malaysia

Acknowledgements

I would like to thank the following people for their contributions to this book:

My team at NCW for their unfailing support: Clive, Debbie and Derrie, Lynne and Rodney, Arthur, Grace and Fern.

Debbie and Ian for the provision of MDF blanks.

Karl for his help and support base coating.

My editor Clare for her patience, understanding and guidance and Shona for her superb photography.

I would like to thank my sister Zoe; only she knows how much I rely on her. The phrase "sisters by birth, friends by choice" must simply have been written for her. There are no words that truly express how much she means to me. But most of all, my most ardent fan and supporter my Dad simply for being there.

And lastly this book is for everyone who shares the love of painting.

Contents

Projects

Introduction

Welcome to the world of decorative painting. Have you ever admired a piece of painted furniture or stopped to study a beautiful painting and wondered how you could recreate the image using paint?

I have been painting for 15 years and the fascination has never worn off. When I open a new bottle of paint I am like a child at Christmas, excited to see if the colour is just the one I need to complete my picture. My mind is always racing with ideas, colours and images. I always carry a camera with me so I can capture some of the lovely things around me, from sunflowers turning to face the sun to dancing bluebells, bright and fresh from the earth to a field of fierce red poppies or lilies with a sprinkling of morning dew. All these are perfect inspirations for designs.

In this book I have painted fresh and simple designs with easy-to-follow step-by-step instructions. Most of the projects can be done by those completely new to decorative painting while others are a little more challenging. However, as you work your way through the book you will progress and learn and hopefully pick up some useful tips along the way. My aim is to remove some of the mystique surrounding decorative painting and to open up a whole new world of wonder.

When I first began painting I just concentrated on creating artistic backgrounds or faux finishes, and could never quite pluck up the courage to actually create a design on the surface. It has only been in the last few years that I have gained the confidence to develop my painting skills. I want to encourage you to paint as there is nothing stopping you. The first time a friend, family member or colleague encourages you or praises your work you will have crossed the boundaries into artistry and your creative world will never be the same again.

Perhaps I should finally confess painting has changed my life, I'm totally hooked. I find it relaxing, exciting and completely absorbing. I hope that some of my enthusiasm rubs off a little – now lets get painting!

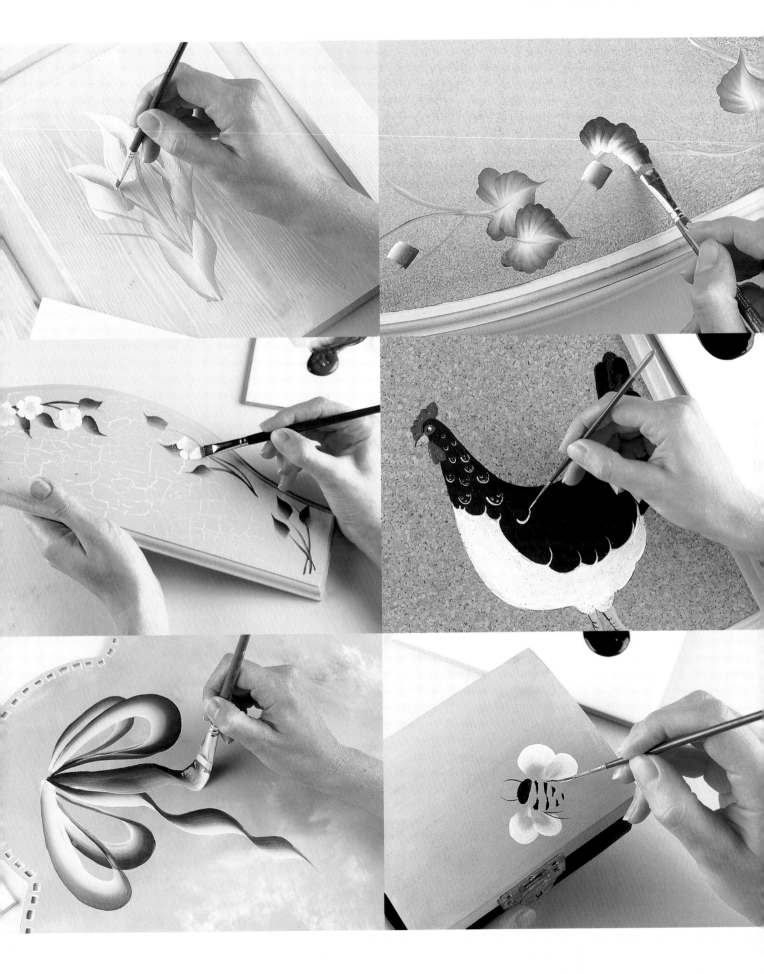

Materials and equipment

To get started in decorative painting you will need some basic materials and equipment. However, much of the equipment you will need can be found around the home so there is no need to rush out and spend a lot of money. Brushes and paints are obviously essential but there are other things that will make your decorative painting easier.

Brushes

Artist's brushes can vary enormously in terms of shape, size and price. Some are relatively good value while others are a substantial investment. There are several things to look for when buying brushes.

A brush is made up of a handle, ferrule and bristles. A good brush should have bristles that stay close together and which spring back freely when pressed into the palm of your hand. A flat brush has a sharp chisel edge. The best way to test a chisel edge is to dip the brush in clean water and run the bristles from ferrule to tip through your fingers. The edge should stay sharp with the bristles together. Round and liner brushes should form fine points.

Brush bristle lengths can vary enormously. The different lengths mean they will act differently. The general rule is that the longer the brush bristles the more flexible it will be and the more paint it will hold. In comparison shorter brushes work better for detail strokes.

The lengths of brush handles also vary considerably. For most decorative painting we hold the brush

close to the ferrule. Good quality brushes have the bristles glued and clamped into the ferrule. If the ferrule is loose the bristles are more likely to shed onto your work; water can also make its way quicker into the brush via a loose ferrule. This will damage and in turn ruin your brushes.

Try not to get confused by the enormous number of different bristles. There are generally two main types: synthetic or natural. Synthetic brushes are much easier to use for the beginner and produce good results – they are also hardwearing and reasonably priced. It is worth spending some time holding and becoming acquainted with your brushes, as your choice of brush can greatly affect your painting. The projects in this book only use a small selection of brushes.

Flat brushes have a flat metal ferrule and should end in a sharp chisel edge. You can paint on the flat side to fill in areas or use the chisel edge for a fine line.

Round brushes end in a sharp point and are available in a many sizes. They are ideal for petals and leaves.

Liner brushes are long and thin and tapered to a fine point. They are used for creating stems, stalks, tendrils and curlicues.

Filbert brushes are similar to flat brushes but they have rounded edges. They are good for base coating and creating leaves.

Flogger brushes are made of very long natural hair and appear floppy and unsupported. These are used to age a surface. To use, first paint your

chosen surface with a glaze, and then using the flogger brush, simply "slap" the brush against the surface.

Stippling brushes are usually square; the bristles are long, stiff and often made of hog hair. Stippling brushes take a lot of pressure so they need to be durable. The purpose of the brush is to stipple wet paint and create a textured effect on a flat surface; it is almost impossible to stipple on a rounded surface. To use, hold the stippling brush in the palm of your hand and firmly tap your wet paint surface with the full force of the bristles to texture the paint. Some stippling brushes come with a handle for ease of use, personally I prefer to get to grips with the brush by holding it firmly in the palm of my hand.

Looking after your brushes

If you look after your brushes they should last you well. Follow these simple rules and you will soon get into the habit of cleaning and storing them correctly:

Dos and Don'ts

• Never leave your brushes in water overnight. They will become waterlogged.

• Never clean your brushes with solvents unless you have used solvent based paint.

• Always clean your brush after use, if paint is left to harden in the brush the bristles will open and your brush will be ruined.

• Never scrub brushes to clean them; always draw the bristles down your chosen cleaning surface.

• Never use your best sable brush for

base coating. I always save my old brushes as they come in handy for base coating. The best base coating brush is a flat nylon.

• Treat your brushes now and again to a little shampoo and set. Remember they are natural hair and will appreciate it. Think how much better your own hair is after a treat.

• Never prop wet brushes up to dry – lie them out until dry and then you can store them. Brushes will dry misshapen and become unusable.

• Use a bar of soap to clean your brushes. Do not scrub the bristles but stroke the soap with them, you can then work the soap into the bristles using your fingers.

Acrylic paints

There is a huge range of paints available now but water-based acrylic paints are the most widely used in decorative painting. They are far more versatile than their oil-based counterparts. Acrylics dry quickly which makes them ideal for the busy decorative painter who wants to build layers of colour without having to wait days for the project to dry. You can use water-based acrylics to mimic oil paints by adding various mediums, or thin them down and use in a way similar to watercolours.

All colours of acrylic paint are made up of a select number of pure pigments. These pigments are made up from the three primary colours: red, yellow and blue. The pure pigments are the same across all brands. Choosing your brand and colour can be one of the most daunting things about beginning painting. A good quality acrylic is smooth and creamy and heavily

pigmented. Avoid paints that sound watery when shaken – you will find that the paint has no real colour or substance. Aim for middle of the range in price and pure pigments, take one bottle home and try it out first rather than buying all your colours as you may find you don't get on with that particular brand.

A manufacturer would take two or more pure pigments and mix them to varying degrees to create the whole spectrum of colours.

Even with the variety of pre-mixed paints available, you may still find that you want to mix your own colours. Colour mixing can be daunting for the newcomer to decorative painting but it can also be lots of fun. Remember that wet paint looks considerably different to dry paint. As it dries it looses a little of its reflectiveness that comes with the moisture, dependant upon the depth of colour it can lighten or darken and give altogether a different result.

Other useful equipment

Tracing paper and transfer paper

These are essential for tracing designs and transferring them onto your surface. Lay the tracing paper over the design and use a sharp pencil or fine stylus to go over the lines. Transfer paper acts in the same way as carbon paper but, unlike carbon paper, it won't leave a residue. It is available in light and dark colours. Position the transfer paper between the surface and the traced design and use a little masking tape to secure it. Go over the traced lines with a pencil.

Painting palette

There are many palettes on the market but a plain ceramic tile makes a good palette for loading paint. A good-quality palette should have sufficient space for at least 12 colours and a good-sized blending area. Most palettes are made of durable plastic making them easy to wash.

Brush basin

A brush basin is a useful item in decorative painting, although a clean jam jar also works well. A brush basin will have two or three compartments and is designed to hold a number of brushes.

Acetate sheets

These are useful for practising brushstrokes and blending and are widely available from craft stores. Simply wipe the sheet clean and start again.

Acrylic sealant / varnish

Most surface preparation requires the use of a good water-based sealant or varnish, especially when painting onto MDF or new wood. Use a sealant when preparing your surface and a varnish when protecting the completed project. Wait at least 24 hours after completing the project before sealing with varnish. There are several options when it comes to choosing a sealant. You can use watered down PVA as a sealant (one part PVA to four parts water), as this is flexible it does a good job. When choosing a sealant or varnish always make sure that the contents are water-based and non-yellowing.

It is always best to apply several thin coats and build up the protection gradually, rather than apply one thick coat. The only time I would apply a thick coat of varnish is if I wanted a heavy gloss finish on a completely flat project, as thicker layers of varnish give the appearance of a mirrored surface. When applying varnish or sealant, do not over brush, as you will work bubbles into the surface. Don't be tempted to go back over an area several minutes after you have applied the varnish as it will have started to dry and you will drag the varnish causing unsightly lines.

Tack cloth

Tack cloths are used to remove dust, grease and debris from wood and MDF surfaces. You can also use a clean cotton or linen cloth to remove any surface grime.

Steel wool

Steel wool is produced using high-quality steel to create a crumble- and dust-resistant wool, which is virtually oil-free and will not leave any rogue strands. Most steel wool is packed in rolls so you can cut convenient sized strips with shears. There are various grades of steel wool for different jobs. If you are unsure of which to use always go for a finer grade. Steel wool is used to prepare old or painted wood surfaces by gently rubbing over the surface.

Scumble glaze

Scumble glaze is a milky white liquid which dries to a transparent finish, it provides you with increased "open time", which simply means that your paint, when mixed with glaze, will stay wet for longer, allowing you to move the paint around on your surface. Many paint effects such as wood graining, rag rolling and stippling are achieved using scumble glaze. You can colour scumble glaze using acrylic paints. It remains workable for many minutes, but once it begins to dry you cannot go back over it as it will begin to drag the paint. Bear in mind when starting a project, that a glaze can take up to 24 hours to cure completely.

Fine grade sandpaper

Preparing items before painting is an essential part of the process. Sanding gives a smooth surface that provides a "key" for your painting. Always wear a mask when sanding MDF.

Natural sponge

Natural sponges are used to create sponged effects, often over a large area. Synthetic sponges do not work as well as they do not have such an open texture.

Wood graining tool

This useful piece of equipment is used to create the effect of wood graining on MDF or other surfaces.

Gold leaf

Imitation gold leaf sheets are used, along with special size, to create a gilded effect.

Paper towel or old cloths

Paper towel is always good to have to hand in case of unwanted spills.

Preparation

Choosing the surfaces

There are many surfaces available to purchase, perfectly suited for the decorative painter. Alternatively you may already have something at home that you could paint on. Medium Density Fibreboard (MDF) is a wood-based composite material that uses wood fibres rather than particles or veneers, to produce board or sheet products. MDF is available to purchase from all DIY and home improvement stores in large or pre-cut sheets. One of its advantages is that it absorbs far less moisture than timber, so base coating is quick and easy. It will also always retain its original shape and is fire- and heat-resistant. Wood glues, nails and staples can all be used to securely hold surfaces together. You may want to experiment and create your own blanks, however there are many companies that supply MDF pieces, ready for painting.

Wood is an ideal surface for painting but you need not be limited to new wood. Painted surfaces can be transformed by simply removing the layers of old paint to reveal the raw wood. You can paint directly onto a painted surface but you should always sand the item smooth and use a sealant.

Safety

Protection must always be worn when cutting MDF; the dust given off has been known to be carcinogenic. This is also one of the best reasons to leave the cutting to the professionals and purchase your blanks already cut.

Terracotta is often used for decorative painting, as its surface is smooth and porous. When painting for outside use an outdoor sealer must be applied after you have painted the design. If you seal the surface first you will be able to wipe off any mistakes easily. When choosing terracotta surfaces, look for those with a clean surface area. Any "milking" or "verdigris" means the paint will flake and often crack.

Preparing MDF and plywood

Always prepare your surface before painting your design.

1 Firstly remove any dust and debris with a cloth. Rub lightly over the surface with a fine grade sandpaper. Wipe over once again with a tack cloth to remove the dust.

2 Next, using a clean flat brush, apply a thin coat of water-based sealant, (use shop brought sealant or use 1 part PVA watered down with 4 parts water). Apply the sealant quickly as at this stage the MDF is very absorbent and the sealant will soak quickly into your surface.

3 Using a clean flat brush, apply a thin coat of base coat. Try not to go over the same area too many times, as you will not end up with a smooth surface. Allow to dry for at least 30 minutes. For best results, apply two or three thin coats of base colour and sand down after each coat is dry.

Preparing old wood

Before preparing any old or unsealed wood surfaces first check to see whether the wood you are painting

has been treated with an oil-based product. Lightly sand the item and wipe all over with a cloth and then follow with a coat of sealant.

Preparing painted wood

1 Firstly, using a rough-grade sandpaper, take the wood back to the grain. You can use an electric sander for this, always exercise caution when operating machinery, do not exert too much pressure onto the wood as you could take back far more surface than you intended to. Once most of the debris has been removed, wash over with soapy water. Allow to dry.

2 If you feel the wood is not quite smooth enough then take a fine-grade sandpaper and gently sand over once again. Use the palm of your hand to judge the smoothness of surface. Once again wipe over with a tack cloth to remove debris.

3 Using a flat brush apply a coat of water-based sealant. Allow to dry.

Preparing terracotta

Terracotta is a very porous surface that will take on a lot of moisture. Leave the terracotta surface to stand in a dry atmosphere for at least two days to dry out before use.

1 Make sure the surface is completely dry before painting. Wipe the surface with a clean dry cloth. Using a flat brush apply a thin coat of sealant over the whole surface area. Allow to dry.

2 If a base coat is required, apply with a clean, flat brush.

Techniques

Now that you have a basic knowledge of the paints and equipment as well as an understanding of the surfaces you can paint on, it's time to start painting! Firstly, make sure that you are sitting comfortably and that you have enough room – there is nothing worse than being cramped. Make sure your arms hang freely and are not resting on the table. Elbows should also be free of the table. You should paint from the shoulder, which means that you will be using your entire arm, shoulder and little finger as one unit in all stroke work.

Loading a flat brush

Correct brush control and loading will make the difference between projects being good and great. Pour out a puddle of each colour of acrylic onto your palette, making sure you have left enough space for blending. Draw the brush back and forth through the puddle of paint, working slowly and carefully. A thoroughly loaded brush will have paint loaded through the bristles. Stroke the brush back and forth through the edge of the puddle of paint. Never push the brush through the paint; draw it towards

you in a fluid motion. The brush should be loaded with paint two-thirds of the way up the bristles. Make sure that there are no blobs clinging to the bristles. The chisel edge of the brush should stay tight and sharp. If it begins to open up this means that the paint has worked into the brush too far and is pushing the bristles apart. If you need to practise a few times, start again by drawing the brush through a clean rag to remove most of the paint. For most brushwork, the brush should be held perpendicular to the surface you are painting on. This gives greater control over the brush.

Side-loading

1 A side-loaded brushstroke has a solid colour running through the stroke fading to a different colour on one side. There should be no distinctive line where the colour changes. Start by loading a single colour onto a flat brush and work it into the bristles. Now dip one corner of the brush into a second colour.

Double-loading

1 Dip the bristles of the brush into one colour, making sure that the front and back of the brush are covered. Now lay the opposite side of the brush into the second colour.

2 The brush should have two triangles of colour. Work the paint into the brush by stroking back and forth across your palette. Reload the brush as before and work the paint into the brush.

2 Work this back and forth to blend the colour, reloading the second colour as necessary.

Tipping

This is mostly done with a round brush to create a highlight.

1 Take a fully loaded round brush and dip the very tip into a second colour.

2 Tap a little of the excess paint off onto a tile. Blend the second colour slightly into the brush.

Loading a round brush

A round brush is loaded in a similar way to the flat brush – you are still aiming for paint two-thirds of the way up the bristles. Roll it in your fingers through the paint – this will gather paint on the brush. Rolling keeps the shape of the brush perfectly.

Line stroke

This is used for painting straight lines. Use a well-loaded flat brush. Stand the brush on the flat edge and pull towards you while painting a thin line. Always use the flat of the brush.

Flat leaf stroke

Double-load a flat brush. Start on the chisel edge and press down while turning and sliding. Start to lift the brush back up onto the chisel edge to complete the stroke.

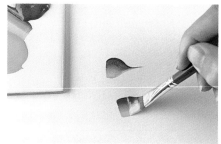

Wiggly leaf stroke

1 Double-load a flat brush. Place the brush on the chisel edge and start the stroke by pushing the brush

down, then wiggle to create a "ruffle", sliding back to the chisel edge.

2 Complete the leaf with either a flat stroke or another wiggly leaf stroke drawn close under the first leaf.

"C" stroke

"C" strokes are used for painting fruit such as plums, apples or grapes as well as the petals of certain flowers.

1 Double-load a flat brush. Apply the chisel edge of the brush to the surface and slide one side a short distance, making a slight arc.

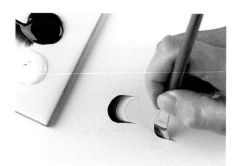

2 Continue into a curve and press down slightly so you are using the whole width of the brush. As you

complete the curve ease the pressure on the brush and bring it back onto the chisel edge, parallel to where you started. This may take some practice as it needs to be done in one smooth motion with a fully loaded brush.

Flower petal stroke

1 Double-load a flat brush. With the brush on the chisel edge, push, turn and slide in a slight arc to the top centre of the flower. Pull the brush in slightly and back to the chisel edge. Complete the petal by pushing, turning and sliding back down to the bottom of the petal.

2 Create a flower by positioning petals together in a circle (most flowers have five petals). A variation on this flower is one where the brush is wiggled on the way up and on the way back down to create a more defined finish.

paint. This will ensure the brush is loaded with enough paint.

2 With your little finger stuck out to help you keep you hand steady, swirl the brush around in circles back and forth and in different directions. You arm must be loose for the stroke to appear natural.

Swirls and tendrils

These are best painted using a script liner brush or rigger. Mix an inky puddle by using a little water to thin down the paint.

1 Load the brush by splaying the bristles of the brush in the paint before rolling the brush through the

---

Artist's tips

Colour mixing If you mix a colour specifically for any project, whether it is for the base coat or design, always make sure you make enough and put the leftovers in a old jar or clean bottle. It is a good idea to make a note of what colours you have used in case you ever need to touch up, or if you want to make a duplicate of a finished item.

Sanding wood surfaces When sanding down any wood surface, whether you are using sandpaper or an electric sander, always sand in the direction of the grain. If you sand against the grain you will in effect score the surface of the wood and cause damage.

Paint stripping When removing paint, I prefer not to use a solvent-based paint remover as this can be damaging to the wood, however on occasion it is necessary. If you must use solvents always wear suitable protection and work in a well-ventilated area.

Varnishing Varnish will remain tacky for a long time, far longer that acrylics. Always ensure any project is left to dry in a clean well-ventilated area away from dust and hairs. Never sand or apply further coats of varnish until the most recent one is completely dry. When working with spray sealers always work in a well-ventilated area or outside and wear the correct protection.

Lace tissue box

This pretty pink tissue box with its lacy design is a delight both to look at and to paint. The pattern is delicate, yet simple enough for an absolute beginner to achieve an exceptionally professional result.

"Although at first glance the design appears intricate, this light and airy look is easy to achieve."

You will need

Materials
- MDF tissue box
- Acrylic paint in the following colours: pale pink, white
- Tracing paper
- Transfer paper
- Masking tape
- Water-based varnish

Tools
- Fine sandpaper
- Tack cloth
- Tile or palette
- 2.5 cm (1 in) flat brush
- Natural sponge
- Pencil or stylus
- 12 mm (½ in) flat brush
- No 1 liner brush

1 Prepare the surface for painting by sanding lightly and rubbing over with a tack cloth. Using the 2.5 cm (1 in) flat brush, apply a base coat to the tissue box with pale pink acrylic paint.

2 Mix equal parts of white acrylic and water and, using a damp natural sponge, sponge over the tissue box by dabbing the surface quickly and evenly. The water in the paint will evaporate and dry clear, leaving a lacy translucent effect. Leave to dry thoroughly.

★☆☆ **Skill level**   🕐 **2¹/₂ hours**   **Techniques:** *Line stroke p. 14*

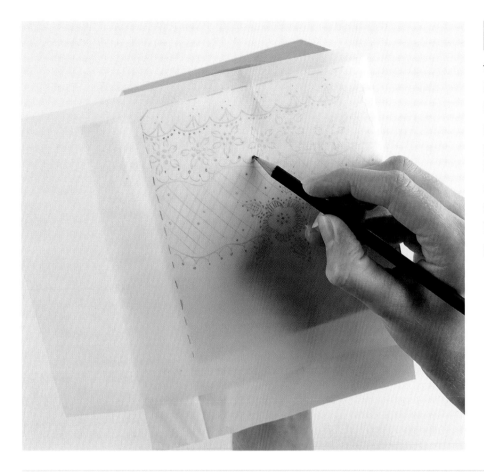

3 Trace the design on page 76 onto tracing paper and then transfer the design onto the tissue box by placing the transfer paper between the tracing paper and the project. Make sure to line the pattern to the edge of the tissue box side and hold it in place with masking tape. Use a pencil or stylus to go over the traced lines. Remove the paper and tape before painting the project.

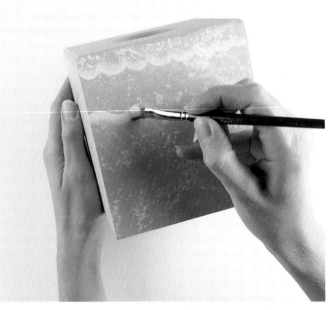

4 Side-load a 12 mm (½ in) flat brush with white acrylic and water. With the white edge to the scallop lines, paint in the scallops. Leave to dry.

5 Using the liner brush, trace in any fine lines on the pattern. Using the handle end of the brush, pick up some white paint and add the dots to the design. Remember to reload the end of the brush to create dots of a uniform size. Leave to dry.

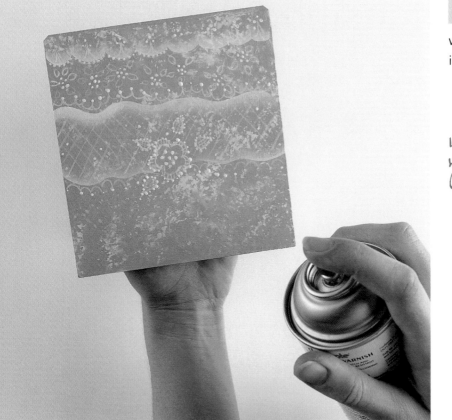

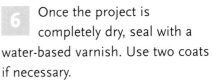

6 Once the project is completely dry, seal with a water-based varnish. Use two coats if necessary.

Helpful hint
When using a spray varnish, always hold the spray can at least 8 cm (3 in) away for an even finish.

Variation

Memory box

This design works well on many different surfaces including papier-mache. Once you have mastered the technique of dotting, why not try your hand at this lovely round box. This would make a ideal gift for storing precious memories. Line the box with fabric for a more sumptuous finish.

Kitchen utensil holder

Ferns are unbelievably simple to paint, beginners and advanced painters alike can produce equally professional results, so don't just limit painting them onto this chosen project. By varying the size and shades of green they make the perfect embellishment for other surfaces.

"To make cleaning this utensil holder easier, use a non-yellowing, water-based polyurethane varnish to seal the project."

You will need

Materials

- Utensil holder
- Acrylic paints in the following colours: light orange, white, Hauser green dark, bayberry
- Scumble glaze
- Water-based varnish

Tools

- Fine sandpaper
- Tack cloth
- Tile or palette
- 2.5 cm (1 in) flat brush
- Flogger brush
- 12 mm (½ in) flat brush

1 Prepare the surface for painting by sanding lightly and rubbing over with a tack cloth. Using the 2.5 cm (1 in) flat brush, apply a base coat with light orange acrylic. Apply two coats if necessary. Leave to dry.

2 Mix equal parts of white acrylic and scumble glaze. Using the same brush, paint one side at a time with the coloured glaze.

★☆☆ **Skill level**   🕐 **2 hours**   **Techniques:** *Line stroke p. 14*

3 While the glaze is still wet, take the flogger brush and drag the full length of the bristles down the surface of the utensil holder in one stroke. Overlap the strokes until the whole area is covered. Complete the other sides in the same way.

Helpful hint

If you make a mistake when using the flogger brush, then simply paint over with glaze again. Always make sure the glaze is completely dry before painting the design over the top.

4 Double-load a 12 mm (½ in) flat brush with Hauser green dark and bayberry. Paint the stems by sliding the brush on the chisel edge, making sure the handle is upright. Lead with the bayberry. To paint the fronds of the fern, slide the double-loaded brush on the chisel edge working from the stem outwards.

5 To fill in the leaves of the fern, double-load the 12 mm (½ in) flat brush, again with Hauser green dark and bayberry. Start at the top of each frond and work down to the bottom. Vary the distance between the leaves.

6 Once the project is completely dry, apply two coats of varnish to protect. Lightly sand between coats if necessary.

Variation

Framed painting

Often the simplest of paintings looks stunning when placed inside a frame. Why not vary this idea and produce your own limited edition paintings. Number each one in the corner with a pencil to add authenticity.

Neoclassical wall cupboard

Neoclassical style offers something a little more refined and, with striking motifs as its signature elements, the stunning design on this wall cupboard epitomizes all things elegant and timeless. The motif on the top of the cupboard is repeated inside.

"When transferring the design don't worry about the detail as this will be covered over by base coating. To reposition your pattern accurately, cut out the whole shape and reposition it as a template before marking in the detail once again."

You will need

Materials

- Wall cupboard
- Acrylic paint in the following colours: white, mink, lavender
- Tracing paper
- Transfer paper
- Masking tape
- Floating medium
- Water-based varnish

Tools

- Fine sandpaper
- Tack cloth
- Tile or palette
- 2.5 cm (1 in) flat brush
- Pencil or stylus
- 12 mm (½ in) flat brush
- Round brush
- No 1 liner brush

1 Prepare the surface for painting. Apply a base coat to the inside and exposed edges of the cupboard using white acrylic. Paint the top and outer sides in mink. Leave to dry.

Helpful hint
When base coating in lighter colours, always apply two coats to ensure a good even coverage. Apply the base coat with a clean flat brush. The size of brush should be determined by the size of area needed to paint.

★☆☆ **Skill level**   🕐 **3 hours**   **Techniques:** *Side-loading p. 13*

2 Trace the design on page 77 onto tracing paper and re-size it to fit your project, using a photocopier if necessary. Position the transfer paper between the tracing paper and project, making sure you line the pattern to the top edge of the cupboard. Hold in place with masking tape and use a pencil or stylus trace the design.

3 To paint the design on the top of the cupboard, paint a base coat within the outline of the design with white acrylic using a 12 mm (½ in) flat brush. Leave to dry thoroughly.

4 Double-load a 12 mm (½ in) flat brush with lavender acrylic and floating medium and, with the lavender to the outer edge, trace the outline to shade the whole design.

5 Paint in the detail by loading a round brush with lavender and reloading when necessary. Use the original template as reference for where to put the detail.

6 Finish off the design by adding some white highlights using the liner brush.

7 Repeat the design inside the cupboard. There is no need to apply a white base coat this time. Apply a coat of varnish once the project is dry.

Helpful hint
The illusion of dimension is created on this project using only two paint colours. Take time on the shading, this will ensure the perception of depth is maximised making the overall effect far more striking.

Primrose cachepot

Summer is always here with this pretty yellow cachepot decorated with primroses. Primroses are a delight to look at and an even greater delight to paint. This project also features smoke marbling, a popular decorative painting background technique.

"Finish the edges of the project by painting them in gold."

You will need

Materials

- MDF cachepot
- Acrylic paint in the following colours: sunflower, white, orange, bayberry, Hauser green dark, gold
- Water-based varnish

Tools

- Fine sandpaper
- Tack cloth
- Tile or palette
- 2.5 cm (1 in) flat brush
- Candle
- Plastic-handled scissors
- 12 mm (½ in) flat brush
- Liner brush

1 Prepare the surface for painting. Apply a base coat to the entire project with sunflower acrylic. Leave to dry. Use two coats if necessary for a professional finish. Don't forget to paint the base and inside of the cachepot.

2 To create a marbled effect, hold the metal blades of a pair of scissors over a candle flame. Black smoke will start to rise from the flame. Move the cachepot gently over the smoke, taking care not to hold it for too long as this will make the project appear darker. Leave for at least 30 minutes before sealing with a water-based varnish. Leave to dry.

★☆☆ **Skill level**   🕐 **3 hours**   **Techniques:** *Wiggly leaf p. 14, Flower petal p. 15*

3 To paint the design, firstly load a 12 mm (½ in) brush with white acrylic, then side-load with orange and sunflower on opposite sides. Work the paint through the brush by stroking back and forth on the tile. You can paint the design freehand or, if you prefer, transfer the design on page 76.

4 Each flower has five petals. For the first petal, with the orange to the centre of the flower, pivot the chisel edge of the brush and turn the outer edge while pushing down. Lift back to the chisel edge for the top of the flower and complete the second half of the petal in the same way. Repeat for the other petals.

5 To create the centre of the flower, dip the liner brush in orange and dot the centre of the flower.

Helpful hint
When painting delicate strokes or fine detail, use your little finger to steady your hand.

6 To paint the flower stems, double-load the 12 mm (½ in) flat brush with bayberry and Hauser green dark. Slide the brush along the chisel edge. To paint the leaves, double-load the 12 mm (½ in) flat brush with Hauser green dark and bayberry. Start at the base of the leaf on the chisel edge of the brush and with the Hauser green dark to the outside of the leaf. Apply pressure and wiggle the brush up and down while sliding it along the length of the leaf, pivot the brush as you turn at top of the leaf to come down the other side. If necessary reload the brush between each side of the leaf stroke.

Variation

Smoke marbled roses

This variation combines the traditional look of roses with classic smoke marbling. Smoke marbling makes a great background finish for any of the projects in this book. The roses are created using two "C" strokes.

Floral coat hook rack

This fresh and zesty crackle glazed coat hook certainly jumps out at you. This project is perfect for a beginner as the simplicity of the design means that anyone can attempt it.

"It is easier to paint the project without the coat hooks attached – when the project is complete you can then re-attach them."

You will need

Materials

- Coat hook rack
- Acrylic paints in the following colours: turquoise, bright green, Hauser green dark, sunflower, white
- Crackle glaze
- Water-based varnish

Tools

- Fine sandpaper
- Tack cloth
- Tile or palette
- 2.5 cm (1 in) flat brush
- 12 mm (½ in) flat brush
- No 1 liner brush

1 Prepare the surface for painting by sanding lightly and rubbing over with a tack cloth. Using the 2.5 cm (1 in) flat brush, apply a base coat in turquoise. Leave to dry.

2 Apply a coat of crackle glaze with a good firm hand, do not overbrush. Leave to dry.

CITY OF ... PUBLIC LIBRARY 33089

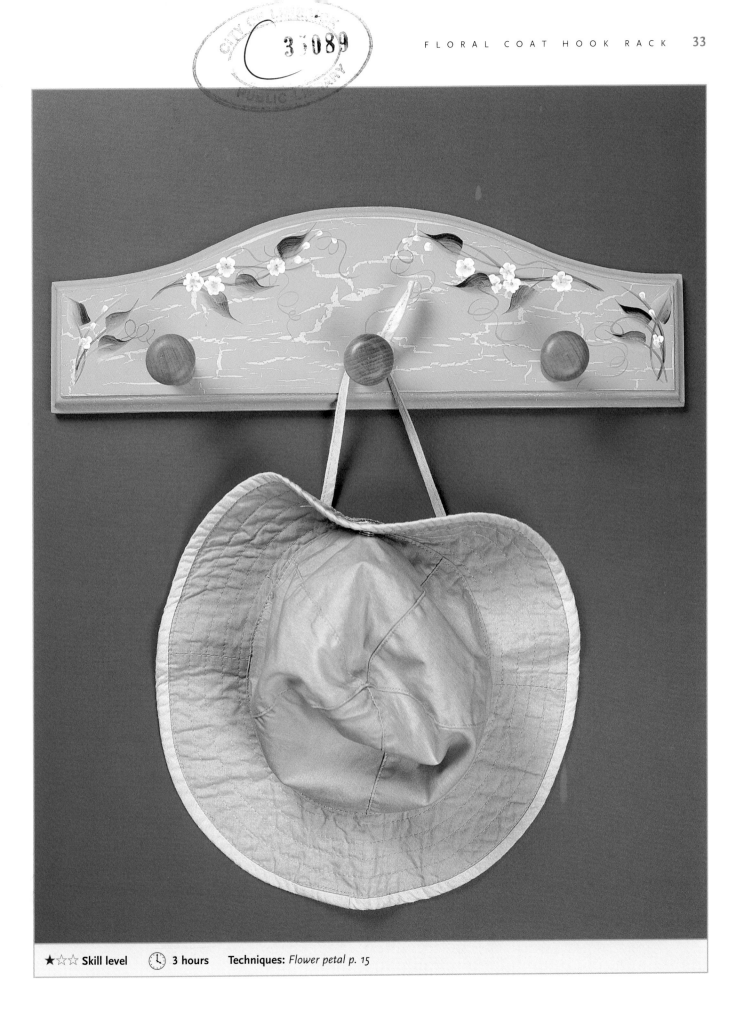

★☆☆ **Skill level**   🕐 **3 hours**   **Techniques:** *Flower petal p.* 15

3 Add a little water to the bright green paint. Without overlapping the brushstrokes, apply an even coat of this green. As this top coat dries, cracks will begin to appear. Leave to dry thoroughly.

4 Painting the stems in determines the position of the design. To do this, double-load the 12 mm (½ in) flat brush with Hauser green dark and sunflower and paint a line stroke by sliding the brush on the chisel edge, keeping the brush handle upright and the sunflower away from you.

5 Next paint the flat leaves using the 12 mm (½ in) flat brush double-loaded with Hauser green dark and sunflower. With the brush on the chisel edge, push down, pivot the brush turning the top colour and gently release the pressure while sliding back up onto the chisel to complete the leaf. Reload and repeat for each leaf.

6 To paint the flowers, double-load a 12 mm (½ in) flat brush with white and sunflower. Reload the brush for each petal. With the brush on the chisel edge, push, turn and slide in an arc to the top centre of the flower, pull the brush in slightly and bring back to the chisel edge, complete the flower by pushing, turning and sliding the brush back down to the bottom of the petal. Complete each flower this way. For the centre of the flowers, dip the end of the handle in Hauser green dark and dot the centre of the flowers.

7 To paint the tendrils, mix an inky puddle using Hauser green dark and water, then load the liner brush. Hold the brush above the ferrule, extend your little finger to improve balance and paint loops overlapping each other back and forth in opposite directions. Leave the project to dry completely before applying a coat of varnish.

Helpful hint
When applying crackle glaze, take care not to overbrush. A thicker coat of crackle will give thicker cracks in the top coat of paint.

Variation

Victorian jewellery box

Even though the flowers are the same, more subtle colours have been used in this variation and the overall look is far more subdued, giving a more elegant effect. To create a softer effect, apply a thinner coat of crackle glaze. This will create smaller, less defined cracks in the paint.

Farmhouse pin board

This project is simplicity itself, fun, quick and really easy; a great gift for a friend, or perfect for the kitchen wall. This bright and breezy chicken design shows that decorative painting is not just about painting flowers.

"Cork is a great surface to paint on, simple, smooth and absorbent. Once the design has been transferred then the enjoyment is in the painting."

You will need

Materials
- Cork pin board
- Tracing paper
- Acrylic paint in the following colours: black, white, red, yellow ochre, green
- Masking tape (optional)

Tools
- Pencil
- Stylus
- Tile or palette
- Small round brush
- No 1 liner brush
- 12 mm (½ in) flat brush

1 Trace the design on page 76 and resize as necessary. Cut out the pattern and, using the pattern as an outline, transfer it onto the pin board using a pencil. For the detail, pierce small holes through the pattern using a stylus. Remove and join up the dots using the pencil.

2 Using the photograph to identify the positions of each of the colours, start by applying the base coat to the chicken using a small round brush loaded with black paint. Leave to dry.

★☆☆ **Skill level**   🕐 **2 hours**

3 Again, using the photograph as a guide, apply a base coat of white. Leave to dry. Continue to paint the chicken by painting the red detail of the head using a small round brush. Next apply a base coat of the yellow ochre on to the beak and legs using the same round brush. Ensure the brush is cleaned between colours.

Helpful hint
Reduce or enlarge the design on a photocopier to fit the surface of the project, then cut out the outline.

4 Load the liner brush with black and add the detail to the chicken feet. Clean the brush and load with white. Add the feather details to the chicken.

5 To paint the grass, double-load a 12 mm (½ in) flat brush with green and yellow ochre. Slide the brush along the chisel edge from the centre of each group of grass, leading with the yellow ochre.

6 Paint the frame using red and the 12 mm (½ in) flat brush, masking the cork off if necessary. Alternatively dilute the paint 50/50 with water for a washed wood effect.

Variation

Kitchen clock

The chicken looks fun and quirky on this kitchen clock. To transfer the design onto the clock, photocopy and cut out the pattern then use it as an outline to trace onto the clock surface. (If possible take off the clock workings before transferring the design.) Try painting other kitchen items for a fun, fresh and co-ordinated kitchen look.

Jewellery box with bumble bees

A completely different look for a jewellery box, very minimalistic, making a perfect gift for someone who prefers a more simple look. Bumble bees are such a pleasure to paint. They are a great accent to any floral design.

" 'Inky black' refers to the consistency of the mix of paint and water. When loading a brush with inky paint, splay the bristles out before rolling the brush though the paint, this ensures the brush takes on sufficient paint to complete the stroke."

You will need

Materials
• Jewellery box
• Acrylic paint in the following colours: French blue, black, yellow ochre, white
• Floating medium
• Gloss varnish

Tools
• Fine sandpaper
• Tack cloth
• Tile or palette
• 2.5 cm (1 in) flat brush
• 12 mm (½ in) flat brush
• Small round brush
• No 1 liner brush

1 Prepare the surface for painting by sanding lightly and rubbing over with a tack cloth. Load the 2.5 cm (1 in) flat brush with French blue and apply a base coat to the lid of the jewellery box. Leave to dry thoroughly.

2 Apply a base coat to the bottom of the jewellery box in black. Leave to dry thoroughly.

★☆☆ **Skill level**   🕐 **3 hours**   **Techniques:** *Double-loading p. 13*

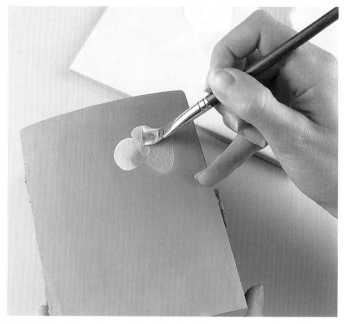

3 Load a 12 mm (½ in) flat brush with yellow ochre for the body of the bumble bee. Paint a large flat stroke starting on the chisel edge and, applying pressure, bring the brush back to the chisel edge to finish at the centre of the tail of the bumble bee.

4 For the wings, double-load a 12 mm (½ in) flat brush with floating medium and white. Starting on the chisel edge with the floating medium next to the body, pivot the brush taking the white round the outer edge of each of the four wings.

5 For the head of the bee, load a small round brush with black and paint an oval shape.

6 Next, load the liner brush with black and paint a thin line for each of the body highlights.

7 Mix black paint with a little water until you have an inky consistency. Load the liner brush by rolling it in the paint and paint the legs and antennae.

8 Load the liner brush with white and paint the highlights on the eyes. When the project is completely dry, seal the base of the jewellery box with gloss varnish. Leave to dry.

Variation

Bumble bee candles

These bold and striking colours lend themselves perfectly to candle painting. Wipe the surface of the candle with a paper towel before painting, this will give the paint a smoother finish and stop the paint from separating on the waxy surface.

Never leave a burning candle unattended.

Herb plant pots

These terracotta pots are perfect for planting out different herbs and look great grouped together on a kitchen windowsill.

"The design is simplicity itself, allowing you to bring your own herb garden into the kitchen."

You will need

Materials

- 3 terracotta pots
- Water-based sealant
- Acrylic paint in the following colours: butter crunch, bayberry, cream, Hauser green dark, grey plum
- Water-based varnish

Tools

- Tile or palette
- 2.5 cm (1 in) flat brush
- 12 mm (½ in) flat brush
- No 1 liner brush

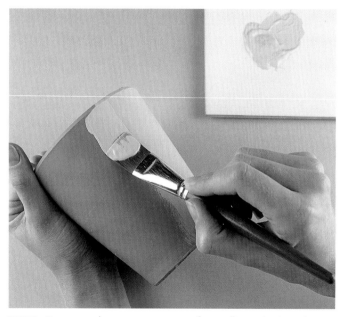

1 Prepare the terracotta surfaces for painting (see page 12). Make sure you seal the surfaces both inside and out. Using the 2.5 cm (1 in) flat brush, apply a base coat to all of the pots with butter crunch acrylic. Use two coats if necessary. Leave to dry.

2 Using a 12 mm (½ in) flat brush loaded with bayberry, paint a rectangle. Leave to dry.

★☆☆ **Skill level**   🕐 **2¹⁄₂ hours**   **Techniques:** *Line stroke p. 14*

Plums and plum leaves tray

The rich colours of summer fruits are a perfect complement to the sumptuous gilding effect that adorns this classical tray. Using basic brush-loading techniques, it is possible to paint plums that are shaded and highlighted in a few simple strokes, creating the illusion that they have taken hours of colour blending, when in fact they can be painted in just a few minutes.

"Vary the size of brushes to accommodate the size of fruit."

You will need

Materials

- MDF Tray
- Acrylic paint in the following colours: barnyard red, white, night sky, berry wine, evergreen, sunflower, gold
- Masking tape
- Shellac
- Gold size
- Talcum powder
- Imitation gold leaf
- Scumble glaze
- Water-based varnish

Tools

- Fine sandpaper
- Tack cloth
- Tile or palette
- 2.5 cm (1 in) flat brush
- Ruler
- Soft brush
- Cling film
- 19 mm (³/₄ in) flat brush
- 12 mm (¹/₂ in) flat brush
- No 1 liner brush

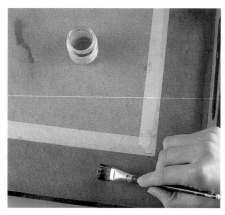

1 Prepare the surface for painting by sanding lightly and rubbing over with a tack cloth. Using the 2.5 cm (1 in) flat brush, apply a base coat to the edges and outsides of the tray with barnyard red. Leave to dry. Mask off a rectangle in the centre of the tray using masking tape and a ruler. Seal the border and inner sides of the tray with shellac. Leave to dry.

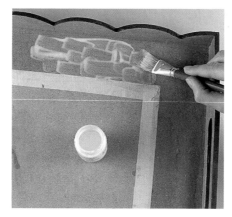

2 Apply a good even coat of gold size to the shellacked area and leave to dry for 20 minutes. After approximately 20 minutes make sure the size has lost its milky colour and has become tacky. Remove the masking tape.

3 Coat your fingers with a little talcum powder to stop the gold leaf sticking to your fingers. Lay sheets of gold leaf over the sized area, pressing them down gently. Don't worry if the sheets overlap.

★★☆ Skill level   ⏲ 4 hours   **Techniques:** *Flat leaf, "C" stroke p. 14, Flower petal p. 15*

4 Use a soft brush to remove any excess gold leaf and leave a smooth surface.

5 Once the gold is complete, apply a base coat to the centre panel with barnyard red, go back over any areas and repaint where needed with barnyard red. Leave to dry.

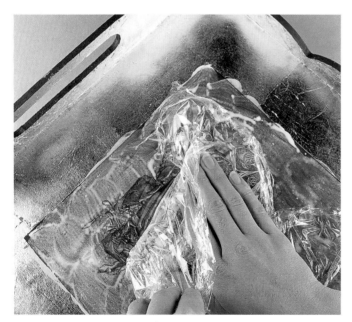

6 Mix equal parts of white paint and glaze and brush on to the centre panel. While still wet, lay cling film over the top, crumpling it with your fingers. Press down. Remove the cling film and leave to dry. If you prefer not to paint freehand, trace the design on page 77 and transfer onto the tray using template paper.

7 Double-load the 19 mm (³⁄₄ in) brush with night sky and berry wine and side-load white onto the edge with the berry wine on. Paint a "C" stroke with the berry wine in the centre. Next, slightly in from the top edge of the "C" stroke paint an oval. Reload as necessary and repeat for all of the plums.

8 To paint the stems, double-load a 12 mm (½ in) flat brush, with evergreen and sunflower acrylic, slide the brush along the chisel edge away from each of the plums in various directions to create the stems. Lead each stroke with the sunflower.

9 For the leaves, double-load the 12 mm (½ in) flat brush with evergreen and sunflower. Place the brush on chisel edge and pushing the brush down, turn and slide while lifting the brush back to its chisel edge. Paint larger leaves using two strokes and keep the sunflower in the centre.

10 Each flower has five petals. Load the 12 mm (½ in) flat brush with white, side-load with sunflower. With the sunflower to the centre, pivot the chisel edge and turn the outer edge while wiggling the brush slightly. Repeat for the other petals. Dip the end of the handle in night sky and dot the flower centres.

11 Fill in any areas with small flat leaves using a 12 mm (½ in) brush loaded with gold. Mix white acrylic and water until you have an inky consistency and load the liner brush by drawing through the paint. Paint loops overlapping each other (practise this first). Once the project is dry, seal with water-based varnish.

Bluebell lampbase and shade

Fresh and simple, bluebells are a traditional English woodland flower. Bring the feeling of spring into any room by decorating this harmonious lamp and base.

"Paint the bluebell flower heads as if growing in different directions to create a more realistic effect."

You will need

Materials

- Lampbase and shade
- Acrylic paint in the following colours: lavender sachet, white, fresh green, dioxide purple, burnt sienna (optional)
- Scumble glaze

Tools

- Fine sandpaper
- Tack cloth
- Tile or palette
- 2.5 cm (1 in) flat brush
- Cling film
- 12 mm (½ in) flat brush
- Filbert brush
- No 1 liner brush

1 Prepare the surface for painting by sanding lightly and rubbing over with a tack cloth. Using the 2.5 cm (1 in) flat brush, apply a base coat to the lamp base with lavender sachet. Don't forget to paint the underside of the base. Leave to dry.

2 Mix equal parts of white acrylic and scumble glaze. Brush this on to one of the sides of the lamp base, still using the flat brush. The glaze will make the white seem transparent.

3 While still wet, lay cling film over the top, crumpling it slightly with your fingers to create texture, and press down. Carefully remove the cling film and leave to dry. Repeat on the remaining sides of the lampbase. Leave to dry.

★★☆ **Skill level**   🕐 **3 hours**   **Techniques:** *Double-loading p. 13*

Kitchen shelf with acorns

This project has acorns and leaves on a kitchen shelf painted in rich greens and nutty warm browns and is designed to improve your shading and highlighting skills.

"Side-loading the brush with floating medium is a great way to shade a project. Use this method whenever you need to create a shaded effect without layering the project."

You will need

Materials

- Kitchen shelf
- Acrylic paint in the following colours: buttercream, evergreen, Hauser green dark, maple syrup
- Tracing paper
- Transfer paper
- Masking tape
- Floating medium
- Water-based varnish

Tools

- Fine sandpaper
- Tack cloth
- Tile or palette
- 2.5 cm (1 in) flat brush
- Pencil or stylus
- 12 mm (½ in) flat brush
- No 1 liner brush

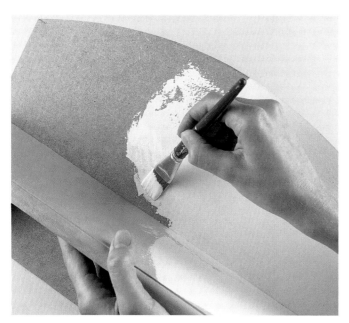

1 Prepare the surface for painting by sanding lightly and rubbing over with a tack cloth. Using the 2.5 cm (1 in) flat brush, apply a base coat to the shelf with buttercream. Leave to dry.

2 Trace the design on page 77 onto tracing paper, then position the transfer paper between the tracing paper and project. Hold the tracing and transfer papers in place with masking tape and use a pencil or stylus to trace the design.

★★☆ **Skill level**   🕐 **3 hours**   **Techniques:** *Wiggly leaf p. 14*

3 Double-load a 12 mm (½ in) flat brush with evergreen and Hauser green dark. With the Hauser green dark to the outside, paint the leaves, using two wiggly leaf strokes for each leaf, working towards the centre.

4 Load the 12 mm (½ in) flat brush with maple syrup and apply a base coat to the acorn cups. Double-load the 12 mm (½ in) flat brush with maple syrup and evergreen and paint in the stems by drawing the brush along the flat of the bristles.

5 Double-load the 12 mm (½ in) flat brush with maple syrup and buttercream and paint in the acorn nuts.

6 Side-load the 12 mm (½ in) flat brush with maple syrup and floating medium and shade in the leaves, with the maple syrup to the outside of the leaves. Reload your brush regularly.

7 Using the 12 mm (½ in) flat brush, side-load with evergreen and floating medium and run the brush along where the nut joins the cup.

8 Mix white paint with a little water until you have an inky consistency. Using the liner brush, paint in the lines on the acorn cup. Add a white highlight on the shell. When the project is completely dry, seal with a coat of varnish. Repeat the steps to paint underneath the shelf if you choose to. Paint a green line around the project using the liner brush. Varnish when dry.

Cupboard with lilies

This small cupboard has been transformed into an elegant piece that will suit any room. The natural look of wood-graining works well with the calla lily design. The lily works equally well whether painted singly or in simple bunches.

"Seal the project with water-based acrylic varnish after the graining stage, this will make it possible to wipe off the lily design if you make a mistake."

You will need

Materials

- Cupboard
- Acrylic paint in the following colours: light beige, cream, bayberry, white, butter pecan, yellow ochre
- Scumble glaze
- Water-based varnish

Tools

- Fine sandpaper
- Tack cloth
- Tile or palette
- 2.5 cm (1 in) flat brush
- Wood-graining tool
- 19 mm (3/4 in) flat brush
- 12 mm (1/2 in) flat brush

1 Prepare the surface for painting by sanding lightly and rubbing over with a tack cloth. Using the 2.5 cm (1 in) flat brush, apply a base coat to the whole of the cupboard with light beige. Apply two coats if necessary and sand lightly between coats.

Helpful hint
For a really professional, finished look, paint the back of the cupboard as well as the insides.

★ ★ ☆ **Skill level**   🕐 **3 hours**   **Techniques:** *Flat leaf p. 14*

Ribbons and bows firescreen

Lavender and lilac colours always work well together. The soft faux background subtly enhances the timeless ribbons and bows. Marbling is one of the most impressive backgrounds and is easily achieved.

"Once the marbling is complete and dry, apply a coat of varnish to protect and seal it. Gloss varnish works best on marble, as it helps to create the illusion of layers by reflecting the light."

You will need

Materials
- Firescreen
- Acrylic paint in the following colours: lavender, lilac, purple, white
- Extender
- Gloss varnish

Tools
- Fine sandpaper
- Tack cloth
- Tile or palette
- 2.5 cm (1 in) flat brush
- Natural sponge
- Badger brush
- 12 mm (½ in) flat brush
- No 1 liner brush
- 19 mm (¾ in) flat brush

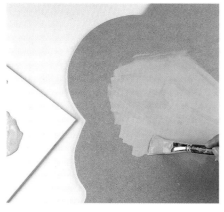

1 Prepare the surface for painting by sanding lightly and rubbing over with a soft cloth. Using the 2.5 cm (1 in) flat brush, apply a base coat to the screen with lavender. Leave to dry.

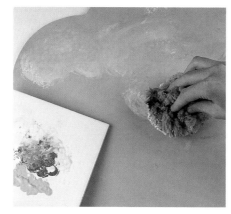

2 Using a dampened sponge, pick up a small amount of lilac paint and gently sponge in a random pattern on the previously painted surface. Intersperse with small amounts of extender on the sponge to allow the paint to bleed.

3 Using the badger brush, brush lightly over the wet paint to soften the sponging.

★★★ **Skill level**   🕐 **3 hours**   **Techniques:** *"C" stroke p. 14*

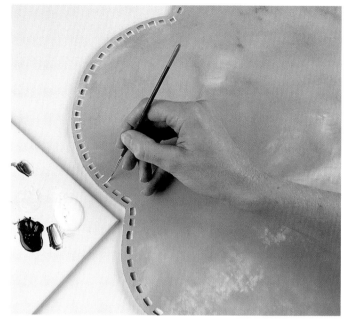

4 Double-load a 12 mm (½ in) brush with purple and white and, following the edge of the firescreen, paint short strokes approximately 10 mm (½ in) long.

5 Load the liner brush with white, paint lines down the start and finish of the ribbon stroke.

6 To paint the loops of the bow, double-load a 19 mm (¾ in) brush with purple and white. With the purple to the top of the screen, drag the brush, applying pressure in the direction of the loop. On the return stroke start to lift the brush so that it finishes on the chisel edge. Repeat the sequence for each of the other loops, reloading as necessary.

Helpful hint
By using a little of the ribbon colours in the marble background you can be sure the colours will complement each other perfectly.